The MONSTER'S GAME

A POETIC LOOK INTO THE CHILD
BEHIND THE MASK OF A SURVIVOR

Written and Illustrated by @LITTLEGIRL413

outskirtspress
DENVER, COLORADO

Outskirts Press, Inc.
http://www.outskirtspress.com

ISBN: 978-1-4327-9764-5

Outskirts Press and the "OP" logo are trademarks belonging to Outskirts Press, Inc.

PRINTED IN THE UNITED STATES OF AMERICA

Prologue

I am an incest survivor. This is the ugly truth that even as I write these words I hide my shame by using an assumed name. I thought about a pen name to hide behind and decided on using my healing name "@littlegirl413." This is the name where I go to get my daily strength.

I live the American dream, yet I hold this secret very close. My abuser was my father, the guy everyone knows as a hardworking family man. He even attended church when we were kids; the loving husband for over 55 years; "Best dad ever" to my baby brother; just the all-round family guy.

The verses in this book express the many feelings of incest victims and child sex abuse survivors. Some are my own feelings and experiences, and some are interpretations from other survivors' lives.

If you are a survivor, please take caution in continuing to the very raw emotions depicted here. I hope that if you continue you will find comfort in knowing that you are not alone, but also that you can find healing and hope. I wish for you to find your child within, and protect and nurture this most precious person. And if you see yourself inside these pages, it's because I am writing about you, too.

If you're one of the fortunate that have not been affected by child sexual abuse, I hope that you will find an understanding of the devastation of abuse and will become outraged for the 1 in 3 girls and 1 in 7 boys who are abused every day. They need your voice.

If you are the loved one of a survivor, I hope that you will find the strength and fortitude to stand by and support your loved one. The only thing worse than the abuse itself, is the rejection of family and friends for disclosure. The betrayal of not being believed and the heartbreak of being told to "just forget about it" are often just too much to bear.

Finally, if you are an abuser--a monster--I hope that you read these words and feel deep remorse, pain, shame and 1000 times the anguish of every victim. I'd wish you in Hell, but I'm too afraid I'd see you there.

Acknowledgements

I would like to first thank my husband, who has not only been by my side for 30 years, but has lived with the many emotional breakdowns over the last years, and especially this last year. He has seen the best and worst and never waivers in his love for me. Without him, I never could have made it this far.

I am so grateful that he is the best father ever. When I look at my son and see him developing into the man that his father has shown him by example, I am so proud. And when I see my daughter look lovingly at her father as only a daughter and daddy can, I am overwhelmed with joy. He has given her what every little girl deserves: security, safety, love, confidence and innocence.

Thanks to my children who are the best I could ever hope for.

Thank you to my "bff" who has held my hand and wrapped me in her arms more than once over the last year. Although I could only share a fraction of my abuse stories with her, it was so important that she remained my friend. Her support has been awesome.

Thanks to all my friends and others on Daily Strength who have listened to my story without judgment. Thank you for the stories you share so that I know I am not alone. Thanks for those DS friends who have read my poems, critiqued them with love, and encouraged me to continue my journey through writing. Thank you to those who allowed me to write your stories and share them as well. Your stories have been so much a part of me reaching my inner child. I am sorry that this is the pain we all share and this book is for all of you, too. Kris, Jessie, Amy and Alyssa, you have all been the best.

Monster[1]

Pronunciation:/ˈmɒnstə/

noun

1 a large, ugly, and frightening imaginary creature:*a monster with the head of a hyena and hindquarters of a wolf a world of fable, inhabited by other-worldly monsters*

an inhumanly cruel or wicked person:*he was an unfeeling, treacherous monster*

humorous a rude or badly behaved person, typically a child:*he's only a year old, but already he is a little monster*

2 a thing of extraordinary or daunting size:*this is **a monster of** a book, almost 500 pages[as modifier]:a monster 36lb carp*

3 a congenitally malformed or mutant animal or plant.

verb

[with object] British informal
criticize or reprimand severely:*my mum used to monster me for coming home so late*

incest[2]

Pronunciation:/ˈɪnsɛst/

Noun[mass noun]

- **sexual relations between people classed as being too closely related to marry each other.**
- **the crime of having sexual intercourse with a parent, child, sibling, or grandchild.**

Origin:

Middle English: from Latin *incestus*, *incestum* 'unchastity, incest', from *in-* 'not' + *castus* 'chaste'

----

[1] http://oxforddictionaries.com/definition/monster
[2] http://oxforddictionaries.com/definition/incest?view=uk

mask[3]

Pronunciation: /mɑːsk/

Noun

1 a covering for all or part of the face, worn as a disguise, or to amuse or frighten others.

2 a covering made of fibre or gauze and fitting over the nose and mouth to protect against air pollutants, or made of sterile gauze and worn to prevent infection of the wearer or (in surgery) of the patient.

a protective covering fitting over the whole face, worn in fencing, ice hockey, and other sports.

a respirator used to filter inhaled air or to supply gas for inhalation.

a face pack.

3 a likeness of a person's face moulded or sculpted in clay or wax.

a person's face regarded as having set into a particular expression: *his face was a mask of rage*

a hollow model of a human head worn by ancient Greek and Roman actors.

the face or head of a fox or other game animal, as a trophy.

4 a manner or expression that hides one's true character or feelings: *I let my mask of respectability slip*

5 *Photography* a piece of material such as card used to cover a part of an image that is not required when exposing a print.

6 *Electronics* a patterned metal film used in the manufacture of microcircuits to allow selective modification of the underlying material.

7 *Entomology* the enlarged labium of a dragonfly larva, which can be extended to seize prey.

verb

[with object]

- **1** cover (the face) with a mask: *he had been masked, bound, and abducted*
- **2** conceal (something) from view: *the poplars masked a factory*
- (of a taste, smell, etc.) prevent the perception of (another sensation): *brandy did not completely mask the bitter taste*

3 cover (an object or surface) so as to protect it during painting: *mask off doors and cupboards with sheets of plastic*

---

[3] http://oxforddictionaries.com/definition/mask

Table of Contents

Chapter 1 The Child
The Monster's Game

She's five years old, but she's not afraid of the boogie man,

Cause the boogie man knows her name.

They said to watch for strangers,

But a stranger never caused her pain.

She'd tell the ogre to go away,

But she's too little to complain.

So while she doesn't understand,

She plays the monster's game.

And now this beast lives in her head,

And is driving her insane.

She can't escape the boogie man,

Cause she knows the boogie man's name.

The Bowling Alley – Georgie's Playground

A safe place for kids to be,
So this is what you believe,
As no one ever seems to see,
When good old Georgie takes his leave.

To up the stairs where kiddies play,
He gathers them around,
And they know not what to say,
When he pulls their panties down.

Now back to his bowling lane,
They don't know what he's done.
Three little girls now feel his shame,
But they won't tell, not one.

Week after week he meets his prey,
Until the night that he is caught.
The parents uttered their dismay,
But what they did was naught.

Now when the girls are forty five,
They all made this pact;
If old George was still alive,
They'd get that bastard back.

***Georgie's Playground* is a true story except for the last stanza. My parents bowled on a Friday night league and kids would play on the back stairs of the bowling alley where George would do his dirty deeds. The candy and quarters that he rewarded us with only added to the guilt we would forever carry.

The Body is Weak

Awakening in the night,

Devil is in flight.

The mind awaits,

What the body anticipates.

Self makes me leave,

To a place of make believe.

Now the body cannot deny;

The soul cannot cry.

The monster has spoken;

The child again broken.

Why does the body lose control,

And give the monster its soul?

Perfectly Groomed

Innocence was consumed as the monster loomed and methodically groomed.

Simple manipulation and complex calculation determined her damnation.

No need to fight for what's right as she receives him in the night.

Never screaming or crying, no denying, she's simply complying.

Secretly, very discretely she gives to him completely.

Then she does awaken, life is shaken and the earth is quaking.

So much shame and blame, she now hates this game.

Not a whore at age four, but what about ten more?

She slowly disappears but throughout the years there are still no tears.

Was it years of abuse or just a ruse, this grooming excuse?

Don't Touch Me

Good touch, bad touch,
No touch can be such.
His touch is too much.
Gotta run from his clutch.

Good dad bad dad;
The only dad
That I had
Made me really, really sad.

Good me, bad me;
That's the V
They'll never see
Don't touch me.

Runaway

No
Stop
Crying
Running
He follows
Disappearing
Nowhere to go
Scared and alone
Returning to home
Monster now asleep
One more night to keep.

***I kept telling him "NO" but he wouldn't Stop. So, I ran out the front door. He had to put his shoes on so I got a little bit of a head start. I turned the corner and saw him coming and I ducked between two parked cars. He walked right past me, but didn't see me because he was looking way down the street instead of right in front of him. I sat there for a long time, trying to figure out what to do next. Eventually, I determined that I had nowhere to go; No one to turn to; Too ashamed to get help. So I snuck back into the house while he was asleep and prayed for another night to keep.

Mommy, Please Don't Go

Please, Mommy, please stay home today.
Mommy, please, don't go away.
I know you're not leaving here to stay,
But I don't like the games that me and daddy play.

Mommy, do you have to stay overnight?
Why can't you come home while there's still light?
I know you think I'll be tucked in tight,
But Daddy does things that just aren't right.

Mommy, can you take me where you go?
Things happen here that you should know.
I lie awake hoping he won't show,
Because I don't know how to tell daddy "no."

Mommy, please why can't you see,
What you did when you left me?
I was alone and scared with no security,
And I just wanted daddy to let me be.

The Lonely Child

The lonely child so full of fear;

If only she had someone near.

She might laugh and play once again,

Just to know she's got a friend.

To Ausie from Littlegirl413

Who is this child whose little heart weeps;
Who lies silently but never sleeps?
Why did no one keep her safe from harm,
And hold her tight within their arms?
This evil that exists, I do not understand;
I reach out to hold her fragile tiny hand.
Please give this child a gift from me,
That she can find some sanity.
We are all here close by tonight,
With open arms to hold you tight.

Ausie's Story

The devil came for her own flesh, her own blood, he was not thwarted.
And the evil one replied, "With coins I'll be rewarded."
I lack a heart to care for one defenseless, so lovely, so good, so pure;
She will find no comfort in this place, I can assure.
So as she sold her soul to the devil for her rent,
She sentenced the innocent to a lifetime of torture and torment.
They cast her with guilt and blame and shame,
That they could continue their evil, to terrorize, to maim.
And the evil ones made her call them names that she no longer understood;
Words with no meaning at all, like mommy, and daddy, and sisterhood.
The child went deep inside of a dark and lonely place here;
The innocent was lost and hope would not appear.
She could not feel at all, not pain, not hate, not fear.
Til one day she saw a message somewhere in cyberspace;
She found her voice there in this most unusual place.
The story was repulsive, but the truth was not denied;
Every mother's heart ached and every daddy cried;
She no longer had to hide the pain deep down inside.
There were no faces to match the words they wrote,
When they reached out to save her with every little note.
And the righteous demanded that the devil release what he tried to keep;
That which the evil one had no prerogative to bequeath.
The devil's refusal led this innocent to the steps with no return;
But all who heard her tiny voice would make this evil burn.
The warriors were angered and linked up their arms around her soul,
Until from this twisted body this child emerged as whole.
The story did not end here as the trauma would remain;
This fear that the evil would return to make their claim.
But when she faced the mirror now, the child that she could see,
Was able to proclaim, "I found her!" "She's beautiful!" "She's me!"

***To Ausie from Littlegirl413* was written for Ausie the first night I met her online. I cried with every word she had written and she had ended her story with a poem. My only response could be written likewise. Still today, I fill with tears for this child.
***Ausie's Story* so disturbed me when it was told to me, that I couldn't get it out of my mind until I wrote this poem. The poem does not begin to tell the horror of this abuse but it was something I was compelled to write for me and the little Ausie girl who told it to me.

The Monster's Boys

The innocence of a boy,

Only a monster can destroy.

Who will ever believe them?

This doesn't happen to men.

Now just shadows on the wall,

They hide the truths that they recall.

Suffering alone from unspeakable crimes,

They cannot remember any better times.

Boys that have grown into fragments of men,

Their innocence questioned again and again.

Questions of who or what to be,

Now invade their sanity.

With suicide rates through the roof,

The innocent shall bear the burden of proof.

You never thought this could happen to men,

But it happens to more than one in ten.

*** *The Monster's Boys* is a poem inspired by an episode of Oprah. 200 men stood together on her show who were sexually abused as children. These courageous men told their stories and it was chilling. It made the statistic of 1 in 6 very real to me. Although I know all of our pain is the same when it comes to child molestation, I also realize that men deal with some additional challenges. I just wanted to acknowledge the men who suffer with us.

Chapter 2 The Secret
The Monster's Test

The child lies safely in her bed,

Not a care in the world, not a worry in her head.

Arm dangling freely from off the side,

She never screamed and she never cried.

When nearly asleep, she feels a hand in the dark,

It was large and monstrous as it reached its mark.

To the middle of the bed she lay without motion;

What was about to take place she had not the notion.

But it wasn't that night that would be like the rest;

What she didn't understand is this was the monster's test.

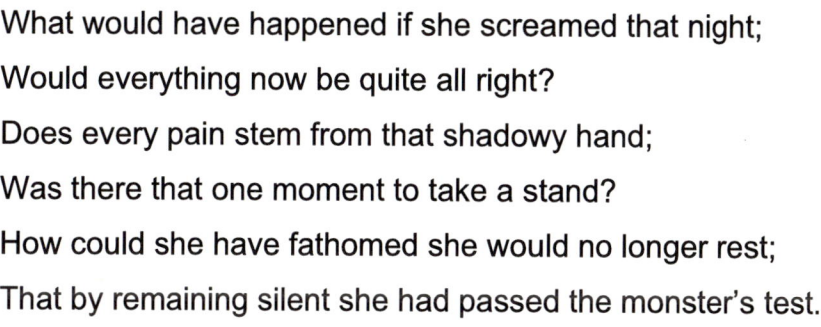

What would have happened if she screamed that night;

Would everything now be quite all right?

Does every pain stem from that shadowy hand;

Was there that one moment to take a stand?

How could she have fathomed she would no longer rest;

That by remaining silent she had passed the monster's test.

Never again would her arms dangle free,

The monster had taken her security.

Now when he returned with his disguise,

He knew he could begin the secrets and lies.

She was too little then to comprehend this request,

But it was certain now, she had failed the monster's test.

***I think *The Monster's Test* was the first time he entered my room. Nothing happened that I know of except that there was this huge black hand down there in the dark and I really believed for many years that a monster had been in my room and it wasn't until I was much older that I realized it was him...he just wanted to see if I would cry or scream. See if he was safe to begin his evil deeds.

Silence

Mountains of words floating inside my head,
Each verse in silence is read.
They are like clouds in Sunday's cartoon,
But conversation escapes all too soon.
A river of emotions flows from inside,
From an ocean of tears never cried.
Sealed in a bottle and cast out to sea,
My speech remains my fantasy.
Alone in the dark on a high plateau,
I scream to hear the prose I'll never know.
But the sentences flow back in reverse,
There's silence throughout the universe.

The Lie

The lines blur,
Not black, not white,
No wrong, no right.
Colors fade into grays,
Nights into days.
The mind says stop,
The heart prevails,
No truth, no tales.
Live or not,
To Heaven or Hell,
I dare not tell.

I Am Here

You're looking at me
But do you see,
No, you only think
You're looking at me.

You're listening dear
But do you hear,
No, you only believe
You're listening dear.

I'm talking to you
But what do I do,
I keep pretending
I'm talking to you.

I'm lying here
But what do I fear,
One day you'll know
I'm lying here.

The House on the Hill

You pass by the house, up high on the hill,
Envying the girl who sits by the window sill.
This secret place within the gated wall,
You imagine the happiest place of all.

I watch from my house high on the hill,
Wishing to jump from my window sill.
Keeping dark secrets within the gated wall,
Dreaming of an escape to any place at all.

You meet the girl from the house on the hill,
Believing she's more fortunate, even still.
But you've never stepped inside the gated wall,
So you know nothing about her, nothing at all.

I am the girl from the house on the hill,
Hiding all the monsters under the sill.
I never allow you inside my gated wall,
Because my life is not perfect, not happy at all.

So next time you pass by the house on the hill,
Just smile at the girl by the window sill.
Don't be jealous of what's inside the gated wall,
You wouldn't trade it if you knew it at all.

Can You See Me?

Does anybody notice me;
Not just physically,
The one beneath the mask,
waiting silently?

Can you hear me is what I ask,
Or is it too difficult a task?
Listen to voices inside my head,
That keep the pain behind the mask.

Can you look in these eyes instead,
To see this other life I've led,
Or keep this mask I've always worn,
To protect the things I've never said?

Can you bear the secrets sworn,
From which this mask had been born,
Or does truth never have a place,
Outside a heart that's full of scorn?

If I remove this mask from upon my face,
To unveil this life that is such a disgrace,
Will you stand by in any case,
And return me to the human race?

Do You Remember, Sister?

Do you remember the monster,
Or could you have repressed?
Do you suffer in silence,
Or have you been so blessed?

Should I reach out today,
To tell you that I know,
Or would you rather forget,
And let the monster go?

I do not wish you pain,
But you must see my quandary;
There is no other place,
To hang our dirty laundry.

Maybe you can't remember,
Cause you were very little,
And I don't know what happened,
Somewhere in the middle.

I wonder if the monster,
You've chosen to forget,
If placed back on your doorstep,
Would fill you with regret.

I've considered another option,
That's just as terribly rotten,
That you are suffering now,
And never have forgotten.

Give me a sign my sister,
That now that we are grown,
We no longer have to wonder,
Don't have to feel alone.

Dare I ask the question,
I dare you ask of me,
Or do I tend my business,
And let the matter be?

Charades

I play charades,
And I am the best at this game,
But I never really win,
Because all I feel is shame.

I play the game with mommy,
I don't think she knows,
I'm really very unhappy,
Although it never shows.

Each day I go to school,
I play it very well,
The teachers never ask,
And I'm sure they cannot tell.

I even play at church,
When forgiveness I would seek,
And at the sign of peace,
I kiss him on the cheek.

The best charade of all,
At my wedding I would smile,
And pretend he is my daddy,
When he walks me down the aisle.

And again today I play it,
As I take a graceful twirl,
Around the room we dance,
To daddy's little girl.

We play charades at Christmas,
As presents are exchanged,
We play this game so well,
Like nothing's ever changed.

At every family function,
I get this game back out,
To keep me from remembering,
What this life is all about.

How will I play when life ends,
And how will I behave,
When people try to comfort,
His daughter at his grave?

I've always hated losing,
It fills me with disgust,
But I continue playing,
To hide the truth I must.

*** I am 52 years old. I am physically ill writing this. I take long deep breaths between each line. My heart is racing and I want to burst into tears. I'm embarrassed when I reread this. Especially the verses about church and my wedding day. How sick was I to do that to myself just to keep the image of the perfect little girl alive? A great big 8x10 in the wedding album to remind me of this sickness. I can taste the bile that is rising from inside me. I would cry out right now if it wouldn't wake my husband beside me. How much longer can I keep up this facade? Will I one day just blurt out the truth to them all? On mother's day this year I almost freaked out when he tried to hug me. What if I had? How would I explain it all? How could I? For now I fear the pain of disclosure not only for myself but for everyone that I love. So I will continue to pretend that everything is perfect.

Chapter 3 Distrust
The Monster's Lie

The father said, "I love you,"

But it was just propaganda.

No need to send out memoranda.

The freak said, "It will make you sexy,"

But it was a falsehood.

Something a five-year-old never understood.

The fiend said, "It would be ok,"

But it was not the truth.

The effects haunt far beyond her youth.

This ogre said, "I'll never hurt you,"

But it was a lie.

Even an adult can't explain why.

The monster never said, "I'm sorry,"

Besides, it would be untrue.

This evil deed, he can never undo.

The Loch Ness

Looking out alone from the shore,

The water reflecting like glass,

I see my reflection staring back at me.

I see the fear I feel inside,

For just below the surface lies,

The loch ness who slithers towards her prey.

Yet she doesn't look at me at all,

But gently stirs and gracefully swims away.

Hide and No Seek

I go hide but they don't seek;
Not today and not last week.
No one looks for quite a while;
So here I hide behind my smile.
No one peeks over here,
Where I hide from my fear.
No one ever looks or cares,
That I'm hiding in my own nightmares
They never seek to find the screams,
So I hide myself in silent dreams.
And if I hide this much better,
Will they forget to come and get her?
I'll bet a dollar if I don't speak,
I will hide but they won't seek.

Hate

Hate
Darkness
Loneliness
Oh, so fearful
It hurts us like hell
And takes away our souls.

Forget About It

You tell me to just forget about it,
But I can't live without it,
Searing images of pain on my heart,
While you deny your part.

You say to forgive and forget,
But I cannot ever let,
Truths die to hide your disgrace,
While others suffer in your place.

Let bygones be bygones you say,
But I can never turn away,
From the shame I have endured,
Forever you can be assured.

You'd like to think mum's the word,
But you haven't even heard,
The worst of this violence,
While you stood by in silence.

I will no longer mind my P's and Q's,
I have paid my earthly dues,
For my part in this crime,
That you wish was all mine.

So go ahead and forget her,
If it makes you feel better,
About what you failed to detect,
And furthermore protect.

Choose Sides

Top side

Bottom side

Outside

Inside

Back side

Front side

Everybody's got a side,

But who's on my side?

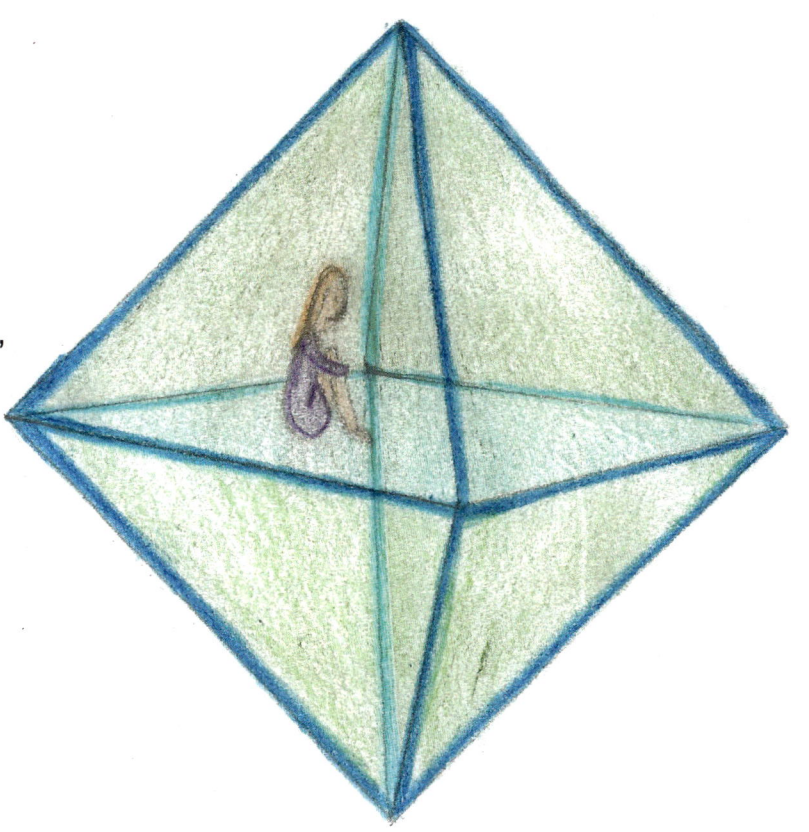

The Dam

The flood gates are opened wide,
Rising waters will not subside.
As people struggle to stay afloat,
Raging waters will topple this boat.
With bodies slamming against jagged rocks,
I don't know how to close the lochs.
I am responsible for their demise,
If only I had continued the lies.
As long as I had walked the plank,
Life was safe on the river's bank.

***The Dam** is what I fear will happen if I begin to open up and tell my story.

Jigsaw Puzzle

These are the pieces of my life;
Many tiny little shapes,
Contours, colors, patterns,
Rejoin into panoramic beauty.
Memories from days gone by,
Where to begin
Patching them together?
Around the perimeter?
Inside a section at a time?
Hours, days, weeks, I obsess
Arranging pieces of time.
Consumes my days.
Covets my nights.
One tiny mislaid piece
Triggers insanity.
Examined a hundred times,
Before I uncover the lie;
A stolen fraction,
The picture never to be complete.

But even as the works unfold,
Do you see the cracks that linger;
All together, but not whole?
Time passes in fearful silence,
The fragile pieces lie.
No glue to bond.
One senseless blunder
Shatters them,
Back into a thousand little bits.
I imagine what is next -
Place them back in their box
Where they once belonged;
Back on the shelf
To keep them safe
From being torn apart all over?
Too tired to pick up the pieces.
Too weary to recreate.
Not enough time to replicate;
Too much time to give up.

Cries

One lonely flower,

Cries out for help,

But who can hear,

Except another flower,

And what can it do?

For it is lonely, too.

Screaming

Deep down inside, there's a person;

Screaming to get out;

I wanta run, I wanta play, I wanta shout.

This person is hiding behind a sweet little child,

This person is a woman, free and wild.

This person needs love without a doubt,

But above all else she needs to come out.

Don't Ask, Don't Tell

I want to tell, but they won't ask;
I'm willing to unveil this vexing mask.
How does such conversation begin,
To reveal the hidden thoughts within?
Would blurting it out be much too bold;
To unravel the darkest secrets told?
Blatant hints are never taken;
Conspicuous acts just mistaken.
If I just start to babble on,
I fear all friends would soon be gone.
No one ever ventures near it;
Too much pain for them to hear it.
If they're too frightened to even ask,
How can I ever remove this mask?

Feeling

Beginning to heal,
Finally able to feel.
Not held in check,
An emotional wreck.

Can't even speak,
Must be weak.
Big baby crying,
Monster is dying.

Finally not numb,
You say it's dumb.
All this commotion,
From too much emotion.

Stuffing it back inside,
To safely hide.
What's bothering me,
You won't need to see.

Chapter 4 The Shame
The Monster's Twenty

The twenty dollar bill I pretended to find,

Was actually a payment of another kind.

I stuck it in my pocket to spend at will,

But the real implications haunt me still.

A gift from the devil for the acts that I did,

My only excuse - I was just a kid.

But still this twenty meant much more,

Made the child into a whore.

I can forgive her for the monster's act,

But not sure I can, for making that pact.

Crimes of Our Fathers

I ask forgiveness for crimes not committed,
My own judge and jury, I'll not be acquitted.
Supposedly free from fault or blame,
Yet I beg for mercy just the same.
I plead for pity on this tortured soul;
A pardon to lift my spirit from this hole.
I solicit forbearance of this debt I do not owe;
Leniency for the condemnation that I know.
There is no clemency in brutality of life,
No understanding, no tolerance, just strife.
I beseech thee to exonerate in heart and mind;
Be benevolent, be charitable, be kind.
My heart is tied and bound in litigation,
While I implore the world for my vindication.
If I am innocent of offenses I've been made from,
Why in the end does absolution never come?

When Red Flowed

Before the red flowed,
A different betrayal had taken place.
But the red showed,
And the monster entered her space.

The red so permissive,
To the monster's hedonism.
The girl too submissive.
To an act that defies reason.

Until the red flows again,
Fear the devil's seed was planted.
And when the red flowed then,
"Never, any more," she firmly demanded.

Now the red flow is gone,
The girl too old and gray.
But the red pain flows on,
With so much shame - still today.

Wash Away My Sins

The heat is intense,
But it cannot cleanse.
The stain still shows,
The blood still flows.
The filth embroiled,
Forever soiled.
The stench will stay,
Never washed away.
The taste so vile,
Of regurgitated bile.
Exit from the shower,
Its water has no power,
To wash away the sin,
And cleanse the child within.

Unbroken

For 11 years the words "No" and "Stop" were never spoken;
The silence was never broken.
It never hurt then, so why does it ache so horribly now;
What right to cry foul?
Where will it lead if memories won't go away?
From right to wrong the pendulum will sway.
What happens to the mind of one without a voice?
Left to wonder now if there really was a choice.
Not to face the pain, the stain, the shame of nightmares,
Only silence and blank stares.

My Shadow

I exist in the shadow of disgrace,
As the sun shines brightly in my face.
My shadow is a long dark path from behind,
Lingering quietly in the depths of my mind.
I disappear into unlit corners to avoid what is said,
Of this dark shadow hanging over my head.
I stomp on this phantom, as if I could erase it,
Rather my own soul should try to embrace it.
As the sun rests heavy behind my slouching back,
My shadow steps out ahead as if to attack.
Never allowing me catch it, it catches me,
Tantalizing and taunting audaciously.
Daring me to step into its obscured path,
I turn away to avoid the shadow's wrath.
It stays to my left, to my right;
My shadow awaits me in the night.
It overcomes me,
Becomes me.
Commits me to the one darkly clad;
I discover comfort in being so sad.
Then I awake with the morning chimes,
The shadow looms over ten thousand more times.

Skeletons in the Closet

Skeletons in the closet
Locked away tight.
Remnants of monsters
Kept out of sight.
Skulls making shadows
Door opens a crack
Devil casts a spell
The child steps back
Bones now exposed
To all those around.
No longer can deny
The mummy now unbound.
The skeletons in my closet
Are just the ones I dread.
Giving up the shadow
For the monsters in my head.

Beneath the Mask

I stripped off my mask,
Appeared from behind my wall.
You drew too near,
Stared too long,
Saw the hideous reality,
And you were scared.
I am ashamed,
Too afraid to look back at you,
That you might read my eyes.
The wall is crumbled,
The mask cracked,
But I want them,
I need them.
You've seen too much,
Stayed too long,
Give me back my mask,
And leave me within my walls.
Go away!
Stop seeing!
Stop caring!
I don't deserve it,
It's just the game I play,
From beneath my mask,
And within my walls.

The Crack in the Door

The lock is latched, the room secure,

Safe behind the bathroom door.

Clothes removed and placed aside,

A bubble bath to safely hide.

Wrapped all up in Turkish towel,

Heart is really sinking now.

The door revealed its major crack,

The monster's eyes were looking back,

Horror quickly settled in,

Where once tranquility had been.

Had the monster looked before,

Beyond the crack in the bathroom door?

Sunflower

Yellow Sunflower,
Smiles brightly against blue skies,
Donned as my disguise.

Me

You are a piece of shit.
I guess that's it.
No, a fucking piece of shit.
Oh, what wit.

So Beautiful

So beautiful.
Mistaken for dull and drab.
In a world much confused.
Used and misused,
In a world who abused.

Chapter 5 **The Pain**
The Monster's Card

I wept today when I received my birthday card.

Why was reading those words so awfully hard?

After years of abuse and sometimes violence,

You still refuse to break the silence.

It says I'm the daughter you love and cherish,

But I feel like the child you left to perish.

It speaks of my generosity and kindness,

Makes no mention of your own blindness.

Truly a card to bring tears to any daughter eyes,

But to me it's just words, that I despise.

You'll Be the Death of Me

You. You own my abuse,
Your hand tied at the end of my noose.
You are the monster, who controls what I think,
You are the poison I must drink.
You are the angel of death,
When exhaust fumes take my last breath.
You give me the strength and the will,
To crush, to swallow this fatal pill.
You forge the anchor that pulls me down,
Under the surface where I drown.
Your image seared on the train track,
Where I lie in wait, no turning back.
You stand behind me on the ridge,
A push for my descent from this bridge.
You hold the match at the oven door,
To ignite the gas that it's meant for.
You grant me the courage to shoot this gun,
When I no longer have a place to run.
You. You are my sorrows, my pains,
The reason I empty your blood from my veins.

New Shoes

Sir, I'd like to return these shoes I wear
For they have caused too much despair.

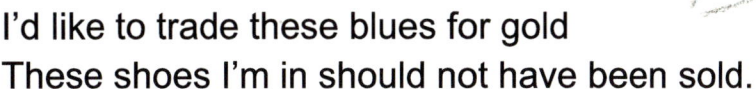

I'd like to trade these blues for gold
These shoes I'm in should not have been sold.

My baby booties were taken too soon
But I'm not asking for a silver spoon.

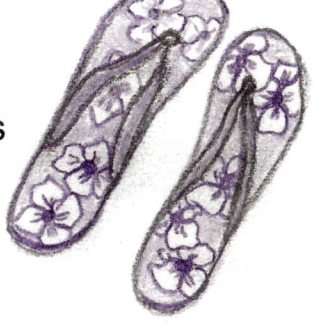

Give me soccer shoes or baseball cleats
Or plain flip flops for swimming meets.

I'm getting tired of being last
I'd bet those tennis shoes are fast.

For wooden shoes just like the Dutch
I sure would appreciate them very much.

If I had shoes for tap and ballet
Then I could dance the night away.

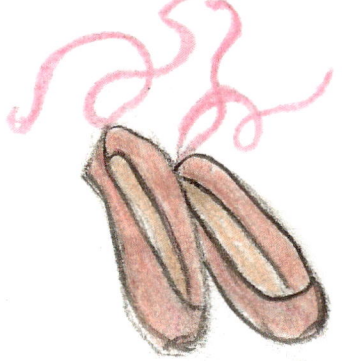

With Cowboy boots I'd dance in line
Or just sit back and sip some wine.

Bowling shoes would slide just right

For my big date on Friday night.

Stiletto heals would make me tall

And take me to the Cinderella ball.

I don't need shoes with lots of bling

I really will take anything.

I'll take those shoes in red or black

But I don't want these old ones back.

I'd even take those ones with holes

If I could trade these worn out souls.

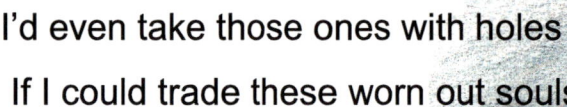

They all say these shoes are fine

But they have never walked in mine.

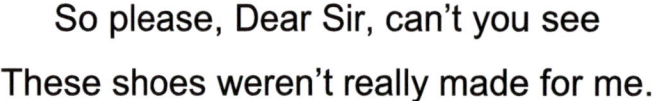

So please, Dear Sir, can't you see

These shoes weren't really made for me.

One More Week

In just one week, it could all be done,
Obligatory roles played out by everyone.
Deep below, the corpse to rotten,
All too soon to be forgotten.
Few will shed their dutiful tears,
An occasional story over the years.
All eulogies would be spoken,
No promises could be broken.
Should have ended a week ago,
Would have been the star of the show.
But the cowardice hides in her lies,
Walks amidst them with zombie eyes.
One more week still ahead,
Another lifetime yet to dread.

Sunday	Monday	Tuesday	Wednesday	Thursday	Friday	Saturday
The End	Morgue	Autopsy	Viewing	Funeral	Forgotten	The Beginning

First Cut

The razors edge across the grain,
Sweet red drips like drops of rain,
I knowingly deign,
This ritual judged arcane.

These scars to explain,
A sensation so insane,
I can only remain,
On this path I've lain.

Quite apparently inane,
But nonetheless profane,
No more inhumane,
Than cries taken in vain.

Observing the plasma drain,
The first cut shall reign,
The subsequent shall wane,
As another breaks the plane.

No feeling of disdain,
As nearer to my vein,
I press, but I feign,
This shall not be my bane.

Another incision to maintain,
A high too much like cocaine,
I try unsuccessfully to sustain,
In the numbness of my brain.

Complete control I regain,
No loss, no gain,
No monster slain,
For right now I abstain.

I'll not complain,
If I break this chain,
But, Oh what beautiful pain,
How lovely to feel again.

Dead Butterflies

I watch the pain

As it flows from my veins

In lovely streams of crimson red

The butterfly now dead.

Sensation absent on my skin

As the blade breaks in

Beckoning closer, more deep,

Yet afflicted I do not weep.

Feeling something more

Like nothing known before,

I let the river flow free

Til I no longer feel me.

Solo Flight

Closer and closer the crowd draws near,
More and more desperate things appear.
They'll never catch me and get inside,
Faster and faster I'll run and hide.
It's not who cares but who can understand,
That can hear the solo amidst the band.
It's the one whose love that I trust the most,
That haunts my thoughts like Marilyn's ghost.
From them I cannot run away,
They're in my heart, they're forced to stay.
I love them more than life, than air,
But they cannot know this great despair.
I need a space both silent and vast,
Where I may make my peace at last.
Do I dare to think of a solo flight,
Away past the clouds and into the light?
Away to the heavens, beyond the sky,
I long for a friend to hear my cry.
Take away lonely, take away pain,
For all I know it's all in vain.
Why do I wonder and why do I care,
There must be more than this out there.
But for now I'll have to sit and ponder,
What's beyond the great blue yonder.
When I am there and I'm the only,
I'll be alone but I won't be lonely.
Now from this fantasy I must awake,
Before I make some great mistake.

Not Just a Junky

They see her on the street
And turn their heads, disgusted;
Another low-life junky
That never can be trusted.
But that's all they can see
From their perfectly narrow world;
They've no idea how
This tragic life unfurled.

I watch her on the corner
And count her endless tracks;
Each puncture is a memory;
Wounds for her flashbacks.
I know the little girl
Who once was in those eyes.
I ache for each betrayal;
This mother's heart cries.

She looks upon herself
In the mirrored glass at the mall.
Reminded once again
Of the shame when she was small.
Back to the alley she hurries
To get her medication.
Hoping this will be the time
It's the deadly combination.

So when you walk beside her
While on your merry way,
Don't judge what you see
Standing there today.
Behind this distorted picture
There's a child that doesn't show.
One that's badly hurting
More than you could ever know.

Undeserving

It's all fine,
For now,
But, I will not,
Survive somehow.
I am undeserving,
This cannot last.
All that is good,
Soon must pass.
I will hang on,
A little longer,
At least until,
I am stronger.

Alone in a Crowd

Not alone,
Just lonely.
Yes, there are people,
But they're quite unaware,
That she needs their attention,
Their love and their care.

The people have gone,
And she's left alone.
But the more lonely she becomes,
The more crowded she feels.
For now she is surrounded,
By vast uncertainty.
As confusion moves in,
She fights it off,
But it must always win.

Lonely,
And crowded too;
Lonely for love and care,
And crowed by deep despair.

The Devil's Plot

Depression,
No repression.
Memory will not fail,
Recalling every detail.
Stuffing the feeling,
It's too revealing.
Denying pain,
Staying sane.
Or maybe not,
The devil's plot.

The Interview

If I despair
While in your chair
You always care.

When you sit there
You cannot share
The pain you wear.

You do not dare
To let fear impair
What you declare.

I can swear
That life's not fair
And trust is rare.

But I'll be there
So you can bear
What's in your chair.

***The Interview* was written after viewing a video of Andrew Vachss with Oprah. What resonated with me was that Andrew pointed out to Oprah that if anyone came on her show she would be angry for them but that she can't be angry for herself. This is the truth that I hear from every survivor that I know. We can believe in the innocence of others but somehow we were still to blame for the abuse done to us

End of a Nightmare

Drawing pictures on the walls of her cell,
Depicting her hell.
White coats come to drag her away,
Refusing to hear what she cannot say.

The scars that tell her story,
Are overlooked in the flurry.
Trying to avert her own rage,
She's locked in her cage.

Sent back to live with her nightmares,
As if no one cares.
Another attempt to end the tale,
Only this time she does not fail.

I Cry Alone

I cry alone, in the dark, in the night,
Silently, my pain, I hide out of sight.
I cry alone, as alone, I must weep,
Always protecting these secrets that I keep.
I cry alone, amongst the noisy crowds,
With the happiest of faces, my weary smile allows.
I cry alone, with the demons in my head,
No more tears at all, as too many have been shed.

Internal War

It's so loud inside--
These voices screaming,
Explosions,
Tears are streaming.
Running, running, running,
Gotta get out of here.
Frozen in this place,
This hell I fear.

A Place to Hide

If I should want to disappear,

Where would I go from here?

Deep inside myself I hide,

To find the child who never cried.

The reasons why I can't be sure,

But in secret, the pain I endure.

If I should shout across the sea,

Would anyone ever hear me?

The Fight

In humiliation, I cower,
I disappear under your power.
Your words cut sharper than knives,
Deeper into past lives.
I shrink into nothingness,
Reminded of my worthlessness.
Unable to stand against the cold wind,
I lie down as if it were I who sinned.
I wish for darker nights,
To end the viciousness of fights.
But freedom has its price,
I do not roll my dice.
I submit to you all the power,
Because I fear the toppling tower.

Tired

Tired.
I want to lie down now.
What forces take me thru the night,
Into daylight?
Too tired,
To go thru another day.
Looking to hang my weary head,
Not yet dead.
So tired.
I'll rest here awhile.
Should I not arise,
Please close my darkened eyes.

Sleep

Wake up, wake up!
"I can't," she said.
"I hear this voice here in my head."
Wake up, wake up!
Turn out the light,
I can't awake this late at night.
Wake up, wake up!
No light, tis day.
Please, please don't end this way.
But I can't wake to save my life.
Please say good night,
Your darling wife.

Awake

You should sleep,
The night won't keep.
But it is the night,
That makes me weep.

Turn out the light,
It'll be all right.
But what's at stake,
If it ends tonight.

You should wake,
The day will break.
But it is the day,
I cannot take.

You should say,
A prayer today,
That I can see,
Another way.

Multiple Lives to Live

Always together, sometimes apart,
Conjoined in life, one shared heart.
A little girl so defenseless,
Another life that's just as senseless.
One protects and one destroys,
She likes girls and she likes boys.
One is a child full of tears,
The other's soul is full of fears.
She tells the truth and she cries,
But the other hides within her lies.
There's one to scream, holler and yell,
The other to deliver her to Hell.
She likes humor, and she's so serious,
One is sane, another delirious.
Distinctly different, indistinctly one,
These fragments of life, all undone.
Fighting to always stay apart,
Struggling to share just one heart.

***Multiple Lives to Live* is dedicated to Rach, Liam, Miss Delilah, The Writer and all in their house.

The Monster's Wife

"If it happened to my child, I would know."

And I laugh.

These words spoken by the mother

Of the child who remains silent after 50 years.

The mother who could not protect,

And would choose denial more willingly,

Than to eradicate the pain of shame

From the child she bore

To be daddy's little whore.

Nothing Less Than Success

You look at me,
And you see,
A success,
Nothing less.

You're so proud,
Like you're allowed.
Living in blinded bliss,
Conscience gone amiss.

Absolved from all sin,
By my humiliation.
Must not have been too bad,
This nightmare life we had.

Because after all,
I did not fall.
I beat the odds,
Your win, not God's.

This American dream,
Makes me scream,
At the secrets still hidden,
The pain forbidden.

While you look at me,
And only see,
Nothing less,
Than my success.

Never Tell Again

You were the first to be told,
And your response was so cold.
It took all the courage I could gather,
But to you it did not matter.
I thought I would be protected,
But instead I was rejected.
I felt in my heart, you thought I lied,
The little girl again denied.
I vowed to never tell again,
These atrocities of men.
For there was no greater good,
If no one understood.
The frigid, bitter cold,
From the first one I told.

Why Lie

He'll lie.

She'll cry.

They'll deny.

She'll die.

They'll ask why.

The Worm

No eyes to see,
They see no difference in me.
Even when they sense the light,
They lack a spine to stand upright.
They creep below the surface of my skin,
Decomposing this carcass of sin.
Crawling deeper into this flesh,
While my heart and brain thresh.
And sleeking out, taking the soul to Hell,
Don't see, don't hear, don't tell.

I Wish You Were Only

If you were just a killer, you would pay a price.

I would not have had to sacrifice.

If you were an alcoholic, they would be very concerned,

About the terrible things I may have learned.

If you were an addict, you'd have drawn some attention,

They would have called for an intervention.

They'd all hate you, if you were a liar and a cheater;

Even call you out as a wife beater.

If you beat me, they would take me away,

But you left no bruises, so I had to stay.

If you were a thief, they would throw you in jail.

And I would be permitted to tell the tale.

But because your crime is so taboo,

They look at me and say, "What's wrong with you?"

The Monster's Execution Is Stayed

The monster was heavy, erect and exposed,

But I could disappear as long as my eyes were closed.

Suddenly, and unexpectedly, he had been caught,

At least that is what I surely thought.

The words ring over and over in my head,

"What the hell are you doing to her," she said.

As she grabbed him by the back of his neck,

I lay silently, an emotional wreck.

What could he have said to make it all go away,

I wondered, as night would turn to day.

The monster's execution has been stayed;

There was relief in being absolutely betrayed.

The true irony is I would have lied through my mask,

But at least I would have known she cared to ask.

*** *The Monster's Execution Is Stayed* took months to write because it is one of my hardest and most painful memories.

One in Three

I am the one in three--

The silent minority.

Not alone in the one third,

We're the ones unheard.

We are but a fraction,

Who have taken no action.

Yet a very large slice,

Who live a tortured life.

I am the one in three.

Who will stand for me?

You are the other two--

So they will listen to you.

Your two thirds have not believed;

The problem is misconceived.

Your fraction is larger than mine,

But you refuse to carry my sign.

You are two slices more of the lie,

You blatantly choose to deny.

You are the other two,

How lucky are you!

The Ultimate Denial

Did no one see her head hang low?

As he entered in the room?

Not one person noticed,

As she led her life of gloom.

Not a mortal person looked in her eyes,

And saw the sadness there.

So she continued to live her life,

As though she had not a care.

Who could ever imagine,

The sadness in her heart;

The depths of pain inside,

That was tearing her apart.

So when the truth erupted,

From deep within her soul;

They could not understand,

Vengeance was not her goal.

They chose to keep this secret,

And continue to deny.

They made her feel ashamed,

And said it was a lie.

Chapter 7 Rage and Outrage
Telegraph to Dad

Dear dad

—.. . .— .—.   —.. .— —..

Stop

I'm sad

.. .———. ——   ... .— —..

Stop

It's bad

.. — .———. ...   —... .— —..

Stop

I'm mad

.. .———. ——   —— .— —..

Stop

Confession to Mother

Thank you, Mother, for my hell;
It's no wonder I could not tell.
You made my life so insecure;
I never thought I was worth much more.

You helped to make me feel ashamed;
I knew with you that I'd be blamed.
I preferred his touch to your rage;
Anything to avoid your rampage.

Do you remember Georgie?
You were surprised it wasn't me.
Seems you were right because,
Guess what...it was.

How could you have made that comment,
Did you really mean to torment?
How could I have told,
When your heart appeared so cold?

Did you know about my cousin, Mother,
And that my uncle was another?
It really didn't matter any,
After Daddy had his plenty.

Were you really that ignorant and blind,
Or did you really not mind?
Or maybe that breakdown or two,
Was because deep down you really knew.

So why is it you, I now protect,
Despite the truth that I suspect?
Or maybe I'm just as selfish as thee,
Maybe I'm only protecting me.

Half a Man

If you were half the man they believe you to be,
I would be the whole woman they think of me.
You get to stand behind a "nice old guy,"
While I stand out front and wonder why.
You sit there comfortably in "Poppy's chair,"
But I see the monster sitting there.
My fault for letting them see a bigger man,
Too ashamed to show I even give a damn.
You may die as strong and brave,
And I may take this secret to my grave.
But the truth is the truth, and the truth will always be,
You're not even half a man for what you've done to me.

Incest is NOT a 4-Letter Word

Whether alone or in a crowd,
Never, ever, say this word out loud.
Pretend it never happened to me or you,
Never say the word, it's the worst taboo.
If no one ever says it, they'll never know,
That national statistics continue to grow.
How do we break this great pandemic,
That's being labeled the silent epidemic?
Stop keeping the secret of family disgrace,
Let's put these monsters in their place.
Incest, Incest, Incest--I've said it'
Say it again, for all those who dread it.
Hey everyone, haven't you heard?
Incest is not a 4-letter word.

Dishonorable Judge

All rise for the honorable judge.
I sit here in anger, refuse to budge.
In disbelief of this decree,
Five years to him and mommy gets three.
Why is incest a lesser crime?
Why does a father get less time?
Any other rapist gets fifteen to twenty,
But if daddy rapes, five is plenty?
Where's the court's mercy for the child in pain,
I look on this sentence with great disdain.
Hold me in contempt when I say to you,
This court assigns children no real value.
This system perpetrates the worst neglect,
For the children it's allegedly sworn to protect.
The case is closed with barely a smudge,
All rise against the dishonorable judge.

Cousin

He crossed boundaries a dad should never cross;
You've given him absolution, now I am at a loss.
Your courage to stand left me amazed,
But your forgiveness just has me dazed.

When father and daughter were about to collide,
They all stood in court on the opposite side.
Now everyone pretends it never occurred,
But I can't help to think this is so absurd.

I watch you hug him and love him and all,
But honestly, he makes my skin crawl.
You're my cousin and I love you a lot,
But you may have forgiven, I will not.

There's one more question I have to ask,
Did you really forgive or is this your mask?
Maybe it's grace that makes you forgive,
But I'll abstain for as long as I live.

The Bitch

Call me names.
I'm the Wicked Witch.
I've earned my right to be a bitch.
Decades of rage;
Inside a cage.
An untamed lion cub;
No mother's love.
Free from the humiliation;
I rise up in retaliation.
Yes, today I moaned and bitched,
But better to yell than to come unhitched.

Reverend BMC

Man of the cloth wherein the demon lies,

How did I miss the demon in your eyes?

The mask of the monster, I should have seen,

Behind the vestment you try to wipe clean.

You were loved, and most of all trusted.

Now the mention of you makes me disgusted.

You wore your priestly robe so well,

As you delivered your sermon in hell.

In the court of man you served your time,

But there is no sentence to right this crime.

I can only hope that this will be God's business,

For me, I grant you no mercy - no forgiveness.

No absolution – you keep your confessions,

No penance for your transgressions.

Your crime may be perpetrated on the body of another

But you have done unto me what you've done to my brother.

You have stained my religion, my faith,

Demolished the one place where I felt safe.

My spirit now daunted and my trust destroyed,

What God had planted, is now a void.

Yet you dare to show your face at the altar again,

Well not on my death will I say to you, "Amen."

Chapter 8 **Hope**

Inside the Mask

A face of rainbows and glitter,
Purple feathered head dress to flitter.
Sweet little lips painted pink,
Long false lashes wink.
The whimsy keeps them from looking more,
They don't understand what the glam is for.
Sad blue eyes deep inside,
Revealing what the mask cannot hide.
A stranger sees the face that's gone,
Beyond the smile that's painted on.
Inside the heart of pain and blithe,
A face that hides the alter's life.

Dear Diary

Dear Diary, Today I am a child of four or five,
Just happy being alive.
Dear Diary, My world changed just now,
Although I'm not quite sure how.
Dear Diary, My life is full of doubt,
I think I'm figuring things out.
Dear Diary, I'm feeling lots of shame,
I'm wondering if I was to blame.
Dear Diary, No one ever hears me cry,
Sometimes I wish I would die.
Dear Diary, I'm all alone inside this mask,
Peace of mind is all I ask.
Dear Diary, I'm fifty something now,
I'm going to find healing somehow.
Dear Diary, Guess I'm not alone,
Just found out what I've always known.
Dear Diary, I told my friend,
There's hope this torment soon will end.
Dear Diary, I'm feeling so much better,
Thank you dear friend for sharing my letters.

Trust

You could crush me,
With your thumb,
But I trust you.
I trust,
Because I must.
To run away,
I'd have nothing.
To stay,
I risk everything.
I remain.
Trusting,
You'll be humane.
Can't leave,
Because I believe,
Your gentle soul,
Will make me whole.

The Lily

So splendid in color,
So perfect in shape.
Swaying softly,
Against the spring landscape.
But in its finest hour,
This flower is cut away.
Inserted in a vase,
And used for some display.
Left baron for winter,
To turn from green to brown.
The bulb to survive,
Beneath the icy ground.
Yet another spring shall come,
To ease the winter's gloom
And give back to the world,
This perfect lily's bloom.

Sun

Sun
Shining
Bright and gay
And with it comes
A beautiful day.

Winter Fades

Very lovely indeed a beautiful site,
This picture I see through the dark of night.
As my heart fills with happiness my eyes fill with tears,
For the loveliest of pictures soon disappears.
Though winter has passed and taken its art,
The snow remains now painted on my heart.

The Fog

Looking into the fog that nature now has cast,
I see haunting shadows of a life that is my past.
Can I bear the truth that's hiding, or is blindness such a gift,
I squint to see the demons, but pray the fog won't lift.
Inevitable forces persist, and the fog now dissipates,
To expose more evil, than my own mind anticipates.
The sun shines slightly across the early morning dew,
Face to face with monsters my mind already knew.
Rising in the skies, the mist is slowly dried,
I want for greener pastures on the other side.
A mighty gust from nowhere, awakes me from my dream,
I lie in silent terror, unable to coerce a scream.
Now in the night I wander, into the fog again.
Revealing all the secrets, I no longer can pretend.
As misty eyes are dried, in the swirling of the wind,
I see through dimmest moonlight, a child who never sinned.

I Am OK

I am OK.
Really?
Is that your delusion or mine?
Look in my eyes and tell me I'm fine.

I am OK.
Really.
We'll all believe this for a while.
Don't look in my eyes just see my smile.

I am OK!
Really!
This is the truth that I hope for.
A soul that is healed, forever more.

The Butterfly Effect

Painted Lady,
Be so kind,
Must have read
What's on my mind.
Sweet Plum Judy
Saves my life,
Diverts the sharpness
Of my knife.
In hopes that she
Protects you too,
I'll name my Monarch
After you.
Gentle showers
Or crushing rain,
My Mallow Skipper
Will remain.
When all my instincts
Start to fail,
I may not kill
My Swallowtail.
White-Barred Emperors
And Cattleheart,
Each will land
To watch their part
When I can't capture one
On my own,
Your Duke of Burgundy
Can make its home.
Speckled Wood
And Birdwings fly,
Today sweet Jezebel
Will not die.

Fantasies of Death

In my sadness I wonder if I could,
Whether anyone else understood.
Too busy to die today,
Not sure I want to anyway.
Only fantasies of suicide,
Too scared to see the other side.

Saving Blue

You're Blue,
But I can't save you.
I once made you smile,
And walked in your blue shoes awhile.
You were still Blue,
And I didn't save you.
I could take every ounce of pain,
And your hurt would still remain.
You would stay Blue,
And I still couldn't save you.
I'd jump in if you're about to drown,
But the weight would pull us both down.
You would still be Blue,
And I would not have saved you.
You hoped I would,
And I wished I could.
But I'm sorry, Blue,
I can't save you.

Ghetto of 1980

Slowly,
We see all around us,
Buildings and people as they fall.
Clearly,
Yet not so clearly,
As the old graffiti that covers nearly every wall.
Drinking and prostitution are taking our women away,
And their daughters too,
For what example have they?
Guns and knives are taking our men,
And when they take our sons,
What have we then?
And our kids,
Addiction and unwanted babies are making them old.
And the only answers we receive are:
"I was scared; I was hungry; I was lonely and cold."
"Please help me!" cries a small voice from afar,
"I want to live…I'll be three t'mar."
But abuse and neglect snatch this one too,
And all shrugged to say,
"What could we do?"
And yes,
That's a baby,
Screaming and crying,
Its father has deserted,
Its mother is dying.
But now as I cuddle this new born babe,
I find new hope,
For a world without hate, or rape, or dope.

The Smile That Was His

Looking out through tear filled eyes,
Remembering that moment,
That slight instance of happiness,
Brought by one quick smile,
Through all that sadness,
And for only a second,
The smile was his,
But the happiness was hers.

And now the memory,
Is seen through the tears that fall
It begins to fade,
But the heart is strong and fights to hold on,
To that instance of happiness,
Prompted by one quick smile,
The smile that was his,
And the happiness that was hers.

It cannot be recaptured,
Nor can it be erased,
And though the tears still fall,
There is thanks in the grieving heart,
For that one brief moment of happiness,
Because the smile is still his,
And the happiness is hers.

Inspired

I wander through a desert,
My creative prowess run dry
Until a rainbow of hope
Catches my eye.

An oasis on the horizon
Is all I should need
To light the fire inside,
My heart shall be freed.

Now I sail on the waters
Of God's great seas
And inspired by beauty
For His Glory, I do please.

Amy's Lullaby

Her many voices have no speech,

No ears to reach.

They quietly taunt inside,

Where all her monsters hide.

They whisper to one another,

The secrets they uncover.

In tongues of foreign lands,

That no one understands.

Into the night their voices ring,

But no lullabies they sing.

Sleep seems not to matter,

She cannot stop their chatter.

Deafening silence will roar,

As boisterous voices soar.

They continue to poke their fun,

As they hear her come undone.

Yet their host maintains her smile,

As the others stay awhile.

Now much to their chagrin,

These voices shall not win.

Chapter 9 Healing
Reaching the Child Within

Little girl, can I look inside?
Little child, please don't hide.
Precious one, can I take a peek?
Baby girl, do you hear me speak?

Little girl, I'm looking in.
Little child, you are my kin.
Precious one, I'm peeking now.
How I wish, you'd speak somehow.

Little girl, look back at me.
Little child, why can't you see?
Just a peek, my precious jewel.
Not to speak, is just too cruel.

Little girl, I saw you look.
Little child, inside your nook.
Peeking back, into precious eyes.
Now you speak, with such reprise.

Now I Can Heal

Yes, I have some feelings,
About all your dealings.
I know this pain,
That drives me insane.
I comprehend this tortured soul,
As I struggle to become whole.
I suffer through this shame,
But I am no longer to blame.
You're the one who is bad,
And I am mad.
I hate the memories you've laid,
From the monster games you played.
I am burdened with a dark past,
But I shall be free at last.
I understand why my heart aches,
Oh, what a difference it makes.
I've learned to feel,
So now, I can heal.

You Made Me a Woman

From a crying infant I arise,
As you wiped the tears from my eyes.
I crawled into your life unable to stand,
And you picked me up and held my hand.
Step by step you stayed by my side,
Traveled with me far and wide.
Then as I learned to find my voice,
It was you who listened, as if by choice.
You never tried to intercede,
Just gave to me all the things I need.
A stronger woman is how I grew,
Because of the love that came from you.

The Broken Doll

Thrown away, put out with the trash,
Her body torn and covered by ash.
Who would want a doll so destroyed?
Whose painted eyes are now devoid?
You looked at her and saw something there,
Besides broken limbs and matted hair.
You lifted her up with gentle hands,
To slowly untangle the twisted strands.
With painstaking detail and reverent grace,
You painted smiles back on her face.
Replaced tattered legs and broken arms,
Crafted repairs with magical charms.
Gradually, washed away the soil and stain,
That she could be whole and loved again.
With new shoes, upon her feet she stood,
Just as you always knew she could.

Soul Mate

You looked, deep into my soul,
And I was scared to death.
Afraid that you might see,
The shattered pieces left.
But you were not troubled,
You did not run away.
You assured this anxious heart,
You were actually here to stay.
That you might look within these walls,
I was truly petrified.
So why were you not frightened,
To reach so deep inside?
Must have been your courage,
That kept you looking in.
How fearless and brave,
You really must have been.
Now you are my hero,
I no longer live in fear.
I know throughout my life,
You'll forever be right here.
Eternally indebted,
For the sweetness of your touch.
I hope you'll always know,
I love you very much.

(For my loving husband of 29 years)

A Sister's Love

A sister's love is like no other,
The perfect gift for one another.
A big sister who loved with utmost perfection,
Never a question in retrospection.

A wonderful story if left untold,
The sister's love with a heart of gold.
But the little sister knew something less,
This family's life was such a mess.

A mother who covered her evil son's deeds
Never considered the little one's needs.
So the story was told so many years later,
The big sister's love became even greater.

A revelation from their simple childhood past,
Now a long dark shadow has forever been cast.
A sister's heart right then was broken,
By secrets kept and never spoken.

Hurt to her core and shocked beyond belief,
How could she offer the child some relief?
Could she have changed the past if she knew?
How should she feel and what should she do?

The sister believed without hesitation,
Now both share the pain and devastation.
The loving sister would have held her tight,
But the child just pushed her away that night.

Because of the sisters' love for one another,
Neither can bear the pain of the other.
With sadness and nightmares they both awaken,
Neither can handle the toll this has taken.

The sisters have become somewhat estranged,
While they ponder the question of what could have
been changed.
The distance between them is more than just miles,
There are oceans of tears, tribulations and trials.

She stands by in silence at her sister's request,
No longer confident she did what is best.
Blaming herself for what she could not have known.
The guilt from her nightmares won't leave her alone.

Surely her sister will come home to her one day,
And this is what she's bound to say:
"That you loved me purely is all that ever mattered,
Because a sister's love can never be shattered."

Beth

Innocent and beautiful and ever so smart,
The devil hurt you and broke my heart.
Still only a baby when totally violated,
Security and happiness now annihilated.

We have failed you, Society and I,
No excuses, no reasons why.
Went through the system without a choice,
Moved slowly through life without a voice.

Promises were made, but only spoken,
And the child within remains still broken.
Left on your own in a life surreal,
Had to turn to the streets not to feel.

No screams so loud as to make them hear,
No punches too hard to make them interfere.
We couldn't protect you from this life you've known,
But I hope that you know you are never alone.

You struggle each day against the tides of life,
Knowing there is more besides the strife.
I wish you happiness, peace and healing,
For what it's worth, I know what you're feeling.

Best Friends

Friend of all friends,
The best friend of all.
Not a dearer friend,
I ever recall.
Whether sadness or joy,
When sharing my news,
You can always believe,
You're the first friend I'll choose.
Chatting for hours,
Or a silent pause,
Whether there's a reason,
Or just because.
I'm happy being me,
When I'm with you,
And I'm even more glad,
I'm your best friend, too.

On a Pedestal

I put you on a pedestal,
Where I could not see a flaw.
But on a higher pedestal,
I no longer saw you at all.
And from the highest pedestal,
You took an awful fall.
No longer on the pedestal,
You're now the best of all.

Cyber Friend

You've never seen my face,
But you see my tears.
Never heard my voice,
But hear my fears.
Never the comfort,
To hold each other's hands,
But you're the only one,
Who really understands.
While we're miles away,
And oceans apart,
You reached out,
And touched my heart.

Sweetly on my heart

You lay sweetly on my heart,
God's own little work of art.
Who mother earth so lightly kissed,
With the sweetest of flowers to ever exist.

Crinkled feet and puckered face,
The Lord has blessed us with this grace.
A cherub sent from Heaven's gate,
Our angel came to celebrate.

While in my arms you lay sleeping,
I cannot stop my heart from leaping,
With a love that cannot be torn apart,
You'll forever lie sweetly on my heart.

****For my first grandchild who brings me so much joy. I love you more than words can say.

Tears for a friend

My friend's grief is hers,
Not for me to know or feel,
My tears for her pain.

Summer Rain

Mist of rain falls down,
Cools summer's heat all around,
How I love the sound.

Rain Dance

Disco lights flashing,
Soft music and loud hurrahs,
Rain dance on sidewalks.

My Hero

My one, my only,
You hold me above the world,
In your loving arms.

Littlegirl413

Little girl Four Thirteen,
Used to think the world was mean,
But it's not, I've seen.

A Happy Moment

One minute happy,
For ten minutes sad,
But it's worth the ten,
For the one we had.

To all who suffer

If guilt haunts your soul,
Turn and face your ghost.
For guilt is but a bully,
Who attempts to control its host.

If in your mind you were wrong,
And in your heart ashamed.
Remember the child within,
Who surely could not be blamed.

If pain encloses you within its walls,
And you can't find a hallway out.
Then take my hand and walk with me,
Together we'll find a better route.

If nightmares keep you wide awake,
Too weary to run away.
Then lay here close to me my friend,
I'll keep you safe today.

The Cure

Flesh of my heart, flesh of my soul,
Sutures of friends making me whole.
Blood through my veins into my heart,
Only thing keeping me from falling apart.
Open my mind, entomb my brain,
No procedure to make me sane.
No diagnosis, no x-rays scanned,
The only prognosis is written in sand.
Magic injections and miracle pills,
No operation to cure these ills.
A stranger holds the surgical knife,
Reaches out and saves my life.

The Ausie Painter

I pour out my heart on canvas.

I am so scared.

Memories bleed from this brush.

No feelings spared.

Simple strokes caressing.

No longer impaired.

Blending hues of natural light.

My soul is bared.

Beauty spills out from nothingness.

As others stared.

Truth displayed in picturesque.

My love is shared.

The masterpiece finally unveiled,

For those who cared.

Want

You want.
I want.
We all want.
But what for?
We've got it all.
It's there.
We can take it…
If we have the guts.

Who

Here I sit,

Under a tree,

I wonder a bit,

Who's thinking of me?

Chapter 10 The Survivor

Unburdening

I'm leaving you along the darkened road,
Now unburdening this heavy load.

No longer any room within my space,
I'm abandoning you in this empty place.

I am hostage to you no longer,
You are strong but I am stronger.

You have made your residence in Hell,
It's my time to break your spell.

You are no longer welcome to stay,
I'm throwing my pain away.

Dear Uncle Joe

Dear Uncle Joe,
Did you know,
What you did at the time,
Was a crime?
Do you wonder,
If your great blunder,
Will be exposed,
And penalties imposed?
What do you think,
Does your heart sink,
As deep as mine,
That you crossed the line?
Can you bear,
Seeing me there?
Are you afraid,
That the hand you played,
Will be the losing one,
As I hold the gun?

Circle of Trust

Draw your circle, round and round,
Within the monster will be found.
He acts so normal, looks just fine,
Stealthily hides within the line.

Watch the children, watch them well,
All the monsters are not in hell.
He'll hug and kiss them, tell them lies,
Then slide his hand onto their thighs.

Teach the children every day,
That saying "NO" is quite okay.
It's totally right to come and tell,
Because not all the monsters live in hell.

A Chapter on Forgiveness

There is no chapter on forgiveness,
Truth lies within this novel business.
This shall be the survivors' rendition,
Victim's liberation in each edition.
Entrusting the reader to not be confused,
There is no intent to free the accused.
All pardons have been omitted,
No amnesty for crimes committed.
Charged - with the nonfiction version,
No excuses for their perversion.
A book thick with the truth of secrets and lies,
There is no forgiveness in the author's eyes.

An Ocean of Love

This love is bitter with the taste of salt,
But I cannot alter this course that leads me deeper into this sea, this abyss.
So deep I can scarcely breathe, but for the breath of your love,
Holding me afloat, like a life preserver around my heart.
A touch like silk-- tantalizing and soothing--I so miss,
As I drift over stormy waves that shatter over the bow.
A kiss that invades my dreams as I pass ships in the night,
And tranquility that reaches out in daylight.
As seas calm and the sweetness of love is my content now,
I wish for this ocean of love to be unpolluted and right, somehow.

Chosen Parents

My chosen mom, my chosen dad,
The only thing that bonds us is the love that we've had.
Safe within your hearts, safe within your home,
You've saved me from the devil, you've never even known.
Never asked me questions, never told me lies,
I was always someone special, when you looked into my eyes.
Nothing ever given, nothing ever taken,
Just the kind of love that could never be mistaken.
Life is so much sweeter; my heart is much more calm,
Because of you, my chosen dad and my chosen mom.

***Chosen Parents* is dedicated to the two adults in my life that I could always trust and who always loved me for me. Mom and Dad D, I love you both.

The Call

I heard Him calling in the dark of night,
My heart was trembling with fear.
And as I lay there stiff with fright,
I felt Him coming near.

His words were kind as He spoke to me,
I listened closely to His call.
The message was clear and I could plainly see,
My past thoughts and deeds had been very small.

He used to be a stranger from far beyond my sight,
To whom I gave no thanks or praise.
But since He came on that dark, lonely night,
I'll love and obey Him all the rest of my days.

Just a Friend

On this day you are my friend,
And this you'll be to the end.
And if our lives go separate ways,
I'll still love you all my days.

Snow

Soft and quiet,
Sparkling and gay,
Tis the snow,
I watch today.

Soft and quiet,
I watch some more,
Tis the snow,
I thank God for.

He Found Me

I didn't find healing through my religion,
But being religious never hurt me.
Getting better was my decision,
But my God did not desert me.

Finding Jesus was not my intention,
When angels gathered all around me.
I didn't look for Divine intervention,
I did not find God, but He found me.

God's Love

What have I lost,
And where has it gone?
I have to find it,
Before I go on.
I don't know what it is,
But I know it's lost,
And I have to find it,
At any cost.
It may be round,
And shaped like a ball,
Or it may not have,
Any shape at all.
I'll search my soul,
And I'll search my heart,
Cause it seems to me,
The best place to start.
But after all my searching,
And in all my haste,
I find it wasn't lost,
It was just misplaced.
And now that I know,
What I was looking for,
I'll never have to search,
For God's love anymore.

Total Love

Love is immeasurable.
It's not the beats per minute we count;
Nor the throbs of our hearts in a lifetime.
No formula for the blood that flows in and out;
No calculation for breaths we take.
For if we do not love with our whole heart,
Is it not love at all?

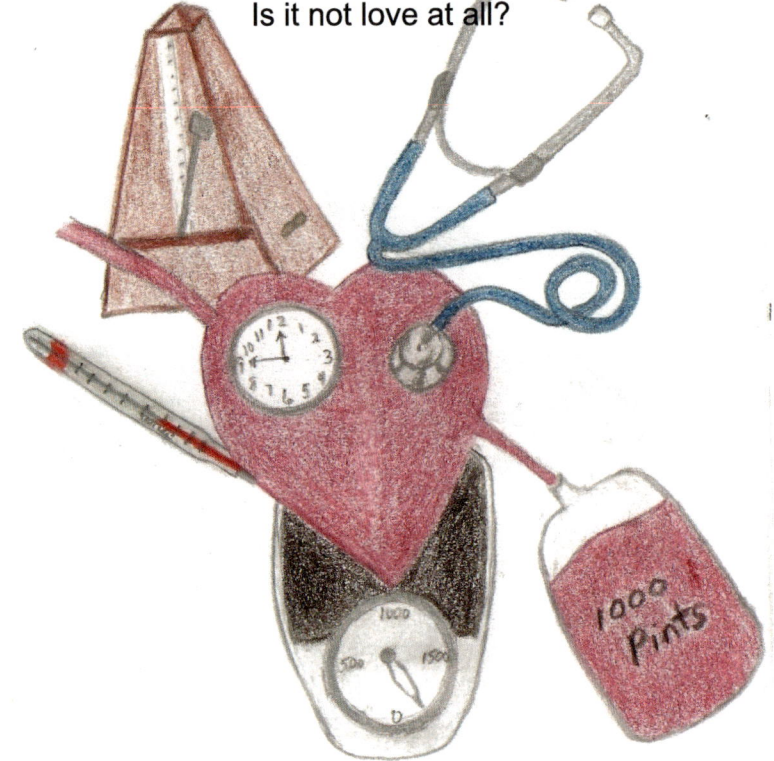

The Monster is Dead

He died today,

And Yesterday,

And the day before.

He can control me no more.

The monster has been slain,

No longer my pain.

I have exited the monster's ball.

I win after all.

Epilogue

I have spent the last year writing things that I dared not even think about before. Through poetry I have finally found a voice. This book started with one simple poem, *The Monster's Game*, which started me on a journey that I could not have expected. I have traveled back into a dark childhood and forward to the hope of one day being free of this burden that I've carried alone throughout my life. I have allowed my inner child to feel; feel scared, lonely, hurt and ashamed. I have admitted the pain and suffering from my abuse and I am able to say it's not my fault, even if in my heart I still can't totally accept that. Through it all, I've become a stronger, healthier woman. I am angry about my abuse, but I am no longer a victim. I have cried many tears over this last year, but I have no regrets. It has been quite a long journey, yet I know there are still many roads not yet traveled. Thank you for hearing my voice.

Survivor's Notes

Your comments and questions are welcome. Send email to littlegirl413@yahoo.com.

CPSIA information can be obtained
at www.ICGtesting.com
Printed in the USA
LVIC092033041112
305804LV00003B